SAGITTARIUS A*

Sibling Rivalry Press, LLC
PO Box 26147
Little Rock, AR 72221

info@siblingrivalrypress.com

www.siblingrivalrypress.com

ISBN: 978-1-943977-78-9

By special invitation, this title is housed in the Rare Book and Special Collections Vault of the Library of Congress.

First Sibling Rivalry Press Edition, September 2020

SAGITTARIUS A*

POEMS
BEN KLINE

SIBLING RIVALRY PRESS
DISTURB/ENRAPTURE
LITTLE ROCK, ARKANSAS

For those who look up to wonder what instead of why.

CONTENTS

Between the constellations Sagittarius and Scorpius, Sagittarius A★ is an astronomical radio source at the center of the Milky Way and the likely location of a supermassive black hole around which our galaxy spins.

Before I learned the risk of expectations
or how black holes warp spacetime, I leaned

over my uncle's telescope mounted like a Scud
in the vinyl bed of his blue pickup,

listening as my mom told my aunt, *Oh,
I named him after his dad.*

My left lashes tickled the aluminum eyepiece
as I searched the sky for Gemini

in that thick, moonless advent,
gloved fingers stirring silver exhalations

that curled like incense, like ghosts
instead of angels. My uncle wanted us to see

some not-famous comet. I wanted to see
the twins that charted my start. *I'll show you*

in the new year, he promised, assuming a future
so soon after Grandpa had become past tense.

I had heard my mom on the phone, whispering
Let's do something Daddy always enjoyed.

I wondered where Grandpa really went, what
he really believed, if he ever smiled, why

I did not know his middle name until I read his obituary.
I named you after your dad, my mom said

over her shoulder, her arm around his waist
as they walked into the night.

FAITH

Gazing up at blue icicles
teething the slanted gray mouth

of my favorite limestone cave
on the farm's east reach, imagining

the Miocene, original mitochondria
curled in the crystalline lattice,

I wonder if they were content
to leave the sea when the lithosphere

and jet streams shifted the sun's chances,
if they wished to twinkle and attract gazes

like buxom sirens on rocks
washed of bacterial advancement,

daring the spectrum to penetrate
their membranes, to analyze their maze

for information they would never
willingly give even as they yearned

to burn by day and tinsel the night
like all the other eyes of God.

Imagine your body stretched in morning beams

like the middle of Andromeda
flattened by eons of virial ache,
its marrow pressed through
dust, fire,
space

curving like fibulas and tibias
back together again
and your fingers reaching

the last light
dissipating in waves
shored outside time. Imagine

those photons settling under your eyes,
in your brow, between your thighs,
around your hips, swinging
from your collarbone, long shadows

filled with bosons, fermions
shoved together again

as it was, as we knew it would be
when we wished we were
taller, better armed, with a brighter
smile, maybe smarter, more receptive
to falling in love. Just

imagine it, fully atomic,
little static fissures, quarks caught
in the lust, returning without
myth, science, philosophies
failed, or magic.

Imagine your body extracted
from our wrinkled sheets,
all those years to begin
again.

FORMATION OF STARS

BOY IN REPETITION

That jut of your left hip flings a wobbly heretical arc as you click through your slides of official NASA photographs, their artificial yellows and daydream blues fooling you, because public domain feels good, noble, true. The infrared originals lack depth or discernable time between you, me, the rest of the room's glowing faces and faraway Sagittarius A⋆. It feels pat, your assertions with research and citations, your obvious selections of gas formations given cute animal names, projected onto the screen like a print of an elephant or a dull map of cow paths across the farm or a flanged orangutan with Griselda tendencies. Where is the endless tesseract, gravity wanting more, more, more? Or do you not believe that? You once told me doubt causes you to feel religious. To spend too much time on your knees. What is your habit? Mom taught us that faith unfolds grace, wonderment, and wisdom requires devotion through more Hail Marys than you could ever hope to accrue. I imagined you with your beads. I warned you. Prayer is just whispered hope unable to penetrate our atmosphere, like the rumored roar of our sun unseen in any of your slides. What is your full capacity? Where do you fall on any spectrum? Maybe you spend too much time on your knees when you should remain upright and promise to repeat no mistakes, to be no bird in the dead walnut tree, tweeting notes of a song broken by the long night with your poor singing voice, to tell them that all color is a trick of visible light and not erasure of faith or fact from plain sight.

We have seen what we thought was unseeable
rendered the orange of an old stove coil.

How else to best portray what is not there
than to use what is: light, color, particular
words like buoy, spacetime, adrift, still
lake, midnight. I might

transform it into a poem about a blizzard funeral,
or a slick thumb tugging my bottom
lip, a waxing crescent
hovering, a quick lover's smile.
Or bags of wet potting soil, waiting
blue tulips, a man undressing
while I watch, a nebula
abandoning shapelessness

to beam into the dark part I imagine
tastes like copper when my teeth forget their roots
and race over the orange, the part I know,

the part they circle on the slide, *This
is a black hole, the beginning
of the end* of all things we can
and cannot name. I might

prefer it continue as a misheard whisper
or terrifying shiver, a ghost, or better,
nothing of known words.

LONELY CODE

Select: Activity Report // unfinished / Select dates // (1987; 2020) // All the times a touch felt like love / total gigabytes per dermal recoil / elasticity : hydration : squirt / [Revise summary]

Filter [smooth] for Z-A descension / (reflection) / useful file://allocation. name / (Query : Where are you?) / Results vary // All the times love fell for sex

Place me between any one / every zero // Repeat into deleted completion / Destination needs no edit : [Click OK] (Are you sure you want to delete?)

(Tapping the *Enter* key :: nothing happens.)

Revise: Transmit into archive / (Query : Maybe through the black hole / go in (suction) go out (bang)) / Even a universe orgasms // Even a god gets lonely (Query : Were you lonely?)

Singular echo pinging to end / Click OK // Copy of [Report on The Number of Times He Touched Me and Meant It] / (Query : When did we last touch?)

(A dream? Rewound / New wound /…healed /…erased) [Error detected]

Returning from 1010 / pulled into adjacency // Disc #2404 / 1010101010111110000000 // matter : energy reconstitutes all manner of spit and marrow

/ longer the touch, stronger the bruise [ERROR] when the fingertips / lift / [Error Report : He is not sure if he wants to continue.] (Will you bounce back?) (Warning : Too near the event horizon, unable to return.)

Click Save // … // Buffer against system failure // (Analysis : Momentarily I am known : (by you)) / Copied for use (/…for what use?) / Read-only / (Query : What is the absence of touch?)

Click X // (Query : Are you sure you want to lose your changes?) [Deletion complete]

Gold beryllium hexagons sparkle
with dead starlight, mirrored chambers
pumping data down from parsecs
ago. With one open eye, I wait
for each filtered image
like scrolling God's Instagram. I wait
as the snaking creeks under my eyes
flood with gin laughter, as brittle crows
linger at the banks, tightening
their grip. After my father refused
to consider a regiment of windmills
hidden from yard or road, to install
this low-frequency radio telescope,
to attempt a third round of chemo,
time stopped. Winter ended
without us mapping the crops.
I didn't decide on wheat or corn
for the floodplain, and it didn't flood
that spring, or the next. I could
have insisted less, listened more. Instead
I harvested most of the timber, experimented
with barley, bragged about right-of-way
revenues. My remaining cousins
still thank me for the two new towers
boosting their signals. We laugh
about the barley. Between blinks,
I watch the stars reveal nothing
about these decades since, their light
hurtling forward, but also, slowing.

ASTROPHYSICS MIXTAPE, TRACK 3

Like "When Doves Cry," gravity
has no bass.

It chirps, a brooding
blue jay when her mate

alights the rim of their nest
with acorns, half

a worm. Not
the thunderous smack

the white coats predicted
when two black holes

scream at each other.
Not the cold head-butt

of one defeating
its mummudrai, an echo

rolling curious heat,
dark matter engaged

in a kiss you and I
picture when he splits

the nut, feeding her,
trembling until she bobs.

Until her next chirp
creates forever.

SATELLITES

There they go: skipping Mars,
bending under the belt
like an agile falcon
to dodge Jupiter's angry eye,
wowing us with a fling
off Saturn's pantheon moons,
dashing past the oblong
apoapsis of Pluto,   still the same
despite demotion.

They report temperatures, degree
of tilts, a lack of wind
between known frequencies
imperceptible beyond the Oort,
data without context, bringing us
no comfort. Nothingness
remains something,
even unnamed,   still a transition
to something somewhen.

TWINKLING

Proteins from chromosome 7 rush to imprint
the blue linger of your lover's thumb
searching your hip and thigh, the dry gulch
he grew accustomed to, and his name
turns a sunset red, like the candle
illuminating your bedroom when you close
your eyes, reaching between his thighs, back
into the first night he undressed in the flicker,
broken beams not suspecting you
are a remnant of before and after
refraction, your quadricep securing
him against you, the troposphere bending
starlight into myths, undulating shapes, maps
you forget when his lips continue upward,
whispering what he learned about forever
while listening to you insist that now and then
are the same, the hunch you have every time
he finishes and opens his eyes.

for AJL

I spin young & baby blue
like the star designated S0-102

boomeranging into its five years in ten hours
orbit all the way through

my arthritic merlot years
faster than the other identified stars I know
orbiting Sagittarius A.

I teeter into proximity, sycophancy
oh so grandly on both sides of
those very good people

waving/smirking/lurking away
from my elliptical state, passing asteroids,
quark ponds, other alien debris

& languorous S8 way out on
their apoapsis, dodging

S14 & their impossibly opaque
ideas about the future as

another version of
our colonized past,   as if
we should ever go back, ever seek
those infant days
turned ashen,   as if
I would not rather know

what awaits after A without sounding
suicidal.   I want
the infinite eucharist of dust
to dust mercilessly squishing me
back into the oldest density of nothingness

so I might burst again,   see
if love remains

so I might begin again
w/ new ideas
if we might call ideas   ideas,
& not gobbledygook
or jabbersnap
          or fusscat because
we might lack tongues

to make sounds to form   words
to make names   to place   upon spaces.

OUMUAMUA

In those brief months of nearness, the astronomers
noted your lack of tail or coma, analyzed your body

for asteroids indentations, trajectory cracks, scorches,
other evidence that you were a craft, not a rock.

They deduced your composition based on colors
reflected as you surpassed Sol's pull, somersaulting

like a neighbor child across our yard. Did you
feel newness, freedom when you departed Virgo

and its autumnal approach to relationships? I wished
they had seen you sooner. I wanted to know

if you were surprised how the heliosphere keeps us
warm, if Jupiter's bitter red eye returned your gaze,

if you anticipated us. I wanted to ask your age,
weight, your sign, your thoughts on Beyoncé,

other cultures you encountered en route. I wished
you could tell us if event horizons are orange

or yellow, if gravity squeals or squeaks, if you
resemble a cock because God likes to keep us guessing.

DEBRIS

Landing parsecs later than our programmed waking,

I craned toward his stasis tube, messaging him, *Can there be love*

without truth when truth often results in sadness. His reply

illuminated the screen of my tube, more red zeros than blue ones,

more empty pixels than known calculus could reorient into a reliable vector

forward. The carrier lurched

like an elephant waltzing, cracking my display, zeros dissipating

into white tendrils, dendrites going dark. Why were we venturing

this risk? He once claimed

history repeats like a lover's mistake you never forgive

because you know time will take care of it. Did I believe that?

I didn't want to go back. I wanted bourbon and fucking, more

sleep, evenings on the porch, clover pinking the yard, but my tube

depressurized, popping open as the ship snapped in half, flinging us

like flares of an upset sun. My suit's nanites

covered my face as I left the debris,

or it left me, I couldn't tell.

the singularity intensifies | my shuttle begins to break

I return to St Mary's | slouching in a back pew
after Kyrie | before Nicene | beyond belief

listening to low incantations of faith upkept
between the altar and me | prostrate bodies

seated | in motion | imperceptibly rotating at
almost one thousand miles per daylight induced hour

that if straightened would span ten lifetimes
recalling | revolving | reaffirming known science

As the lector approaches the ambo | First Reading

triggering silence | clearing her throat | pausing for
eighty unspun miles to see me | her eldest

still green-eyed and lanky | mouthing my name
after decades | many deaths | despite prior promises

to speak no new names | She makes
no reaction | begins her recitation as if I were

never married | maybe gaseous | possibly burned off
like a blue dwarf dragged over the event horizon

Why did I circle back to into this moment | amen

a man | who | what husband | as the gravity
shimmies with its infinite boredom to bring me back

She returns to her seat | upright | in the front pew

cuing the organist | Psalm 23:3 | smoothing her dress
against static | wrinkles | rupture | any shape of change

TO TRANSITION

from when
I used to slip inside
that limestone cave
off Darklick Road,
the start of our property fence
& puberty

& now, I feel my femurs
forgetting their density
their breaking [*   ]

my hayfield skin submitting
to the galactic engine
that pullsustogether by
stretching   us   a p   a   r   t
like the light, seeking

widened pores
as a sieve,   a colander
draining little
bright   concentrated   beams

not snatching crawfish from the shallows
where Pine Creek   meanders
before doubling
back
without betrayal

& a lack of devotion in what was not
what could not
what was lost
what should not   have been
in that cave with him

had I a six-string   or
Grandma's upright,
its ivory keys,   the broken
lower C-flat   or

sufficient ni trous mo le cules
through which
to transmit
my hymns

about eucharist, rhymes small
& crisp at audible frequencies, waves
off my twang

slip ping
at length
be tween
the peal
ing notes

& my liver thirsty for another pour
until I blue   to black
viral bruise spreading
by dull dead uncle teeth

which hold tight
& remind me
that language   we used
before   we used
words, their sharp
shininess feared, held   away
like a blade   we used
to carve

our initials into oaks
& enemies into   pieces
we carry until when
becomes now
again.

HER CASKET DESCENDS

I find a wrinkled Lincoln
double-folded in my jacket
pocket. She planted them

for late night lattes, bus
fare, *those donuts you like*.
She knew. She always knew

leukemia would dissolve her.
I squint, the spray of white
lilies and gladioli sinking,

no roses, dammit. I listen
for sulphides, ammonia,
her methanes sputtering

into the nitrogen and oxygen
around us. I hold my breath.
I brace myself against that

outward pull. Solar winds,
bent light, our arm of the Way
swelling, nebulae flirting

with planets, pulsars, our end
eventually, the only tether back
being what we remember, travel

that so frequently fails
or worse, diverts. I recall her
almond eyes. The casket stops

halfway, swaying like her hair
that August on the beach
before Andrew, my siblings

and their children searching
the dirt like sexton beetles,
archeologists, rats maybe.

Or whatever. I unfold the five
at Ward's Donuts, order black
decaf in white Styrofoam,

a second jumbo Sweet Grease
sticking to my fingers, my gut
telling me nothing new.

FINAL TRANSMISSION

My ears popped when our carbon fiber shuttles
launched from the carrier bay, sailing
toward Sagittarius A★
until a gamma burst   blinded
every pilot   & melted our   hope
    you   messaged me
        reported if   those   stabilizers   functioning
            Sunday afternoons
            we floated   nude
    in tractor tire tubes   under   beams,   the longest
                                                                        days

            we knew   how to count
              we learned   loss
            manipulates   space   time
                                        after
            aluminum becomes   p p p plasma
                after   my fa father   forgot
            & unnamed me
                after   did   not matter
        after   your shuttle   disappeared
                & newly negative   particle s

    absconded   other
    neutral
            s p a c e   as   if
                            flung,

            a rude   boy's sling
                                    as   if
                we   were   his smooth
                  pebbles   skittering
                    across   the
                                                    emerald
    s ur f a c e
                of a   winter l l lake
                un til   we
                                        too
                                            sub
                                            m e rrr
                                                        g e

32

VIATICUM

I have achieved the end quivering
inside the teardrop of a forgotten god
devouring nearby light, shuttle debris,
my grey left boot, a careening shard
of bloody ulna. Time loses meaning
without light. I can't see my supper
flying ahead of me. Did the bread
taste like arugula, candied bacon,
saltines? Did I dream about wine
on my lover's lips? Did he kiss
to the side and have green eyes?
His thumb on my hip felt like a fall.
I can't see my hands unthreading
flesh, fiber, tendon, ligament
to bone. Will the marrow remain
red in this pressure, this kindled
tangerine stretching my lips
too thin to recite one more
Amen? When becomes
where the light contracts,
my aqueous humor forms
bubbles the black hole
ingests. My tongue
dissolves like water
flicked on hot asphalt.
I leave the light.
I cannot see
my teeth
scatter
to ash.

AFTER

When I ask the priest if dead souls travel

to space after light,   he pivots

from my mother's coffin

as if something forbidden

prowls behind me.   Other mourners

return to sedans and large trucks. The day tugs

an amaranth haze over faded headstones, flat grass

browned by melted snow and tires. The first stars

distract us from what changed during the day, revealing

a shrinking,

                    damp clay returned to her grave forming

a mound.   The priest cannot stop blinking.

Light reaches an answer or pivots,

                              we never know

even if they return.

If I were to lob myself
over the mandarin swirl
into Sagittarius A★

when I could be napping
in my uncle's cabin
on a flooded Tuesday,

or catching bourbon in my belly
at The Iron Horse Tavern
during Sunday karaoke,

or meeting some Peter
in the birch thicket
behind the parish cemetery,

would I reconvene
as $CaCO_3$ forming
the tail of a comet
flirting with Andromeda's arms

in that old-fashioned way
old men at the Tavern
turned their gravity on me,

fingertips like lizards
grazing the soft spot inside
my bicep, descending
my vertebrae to my lumbar

in the gold churn
of before, during and after,
the pull feeling brilliant
within every ligament,

or would my mass
convert to plasma spilling
out the other side, because
inertia is eternal, momentum

relies on the light, and men
in shadows always refuse
to stop?

Or would the idea of me
continue like alpha waves,
glutamate vapors traveling
space free of time,

my neutrons seeking
a charge akin to the men
at the windowless afterhours
off Exit 21,
touching the edge

of shouldn't?
Always the men,
their singular wants.

GHAZAL THE STARS

That night in the telescope   I discovered the far stars
are not dead angels   lit at feathered angles. The stars

are uneven men, averse   & akin, like my mom,
preoccupied with fueling   azotic excuses only parents & stars

have the longevity   to sustain, the parsecs
passed uncounted   between any two or more stars

& even more men to prevent   mutually detrimental immolation.
Pants afire, the men   aspire to asking the stars

for what they might remember   & I discovered no stars
sit still, similar to men   who cannot love others, only stars

charting a path to impossible   answers they follow to me, just
another Ben who dreams of men   as angels reeling me in to the stars.

Thank you to the following publications in which works from this project have appeared:

"Ghazal the Stars" in *Impossible Archetype*.
"Boy in Repetition" in *The Mantle*.
"Doubt" in *Pidgeonholes*.
"Big Bang" in *8 Poems*.
"newworldorder" in *Astral Waters Review*.
"Lonely Code" in *Okay Donkey*.
An early version of "Twinkling" in *GRAVITON Lit*.
"The Part I Know" in *The Cortland Review*.

Thank you to the stars and Sagittarius A★, holding us together until the end.

Thank you to Angie Lilly, Todd Dillard, John Byrne, Melissa Norris and Holly Prochaska for their guidance and feedback. Thanks to AJL for listening to me ramble about simultaneous time, string theory and heliospheres.

ACKNOWLEDGMENTS

THE POET

Ben Kline lives in Cincinnati, Ohio. He is the author of *Going Fast in Loose Directions* and is recipient of the Christopher Hewitt Award for Poetry from *A&U Magazine*. His work has appeared in *DIAGRAM*, *Hobart*, and elsewhere.

benklineonline.wordpress.com

Sibling Rivalry Press is an independent press based in Little Rock, Arkansas. It is a sponsored project of Fractured Atlas, a nonprofit arts service organization. Contributions to support the operations of Sibling Rivalry Press are tax-deductible to the extent permitted by law, and your donations will directly assist in the publication of work that disturbs and enraptures. To contribute to the publication of more books like this one, please visit our website and click *donate*.

Sibling Rivalry Press gratefully acknowledges the following donors, without whom this book would not be possible:

Anonymous (18)
Arkansas Arts Council
John Bateman
W. Stephen Breedlove
Dustin Brookshire
Sarah Browning
Billy Butler
Asher Carter
Don Cellini
Nicole Connolly
Jim Cory
Risa Denenberg
John Gaudin
In Memory of Karen Hayes
Gustavo Hernandez
Amy Holman
Jessica Jacobs & Nickole Brown
Paige James
Nahal Suzanne Jamir
Allison Joseph
Collin Kelley
Trevor Ketner

Andrea Lawlor
Anthony Lioi
Ed Madden & Bert Easter
Mitchell, Blackstock, Ivers & Sneddon, PLLC
Stephen Mitchell
National Endowment for the Arts
Stacy Pendergrast
Simon Randall
Paul Romero
Randi M. Romo
Carol Rosenfeld
Joseph Ross
In Memory of Bill Rous
Matthew Siegel
Alana Smoot
Katherine Sullivan
Tony Taylor
Leslie Taylor
Hugh Tipping
Guy Traiber
Mark Ward
Robert Wright

THE PRESS